BEFORE WE GO ANY FURTHER

Tristram Fane Saunders lives in London and works as a journalist. He is the author of five pamphlets including *The Rake* (The Poetry Business, 2022), and is the editor of *Edna St Vincent Millay: Poems and Satires* (Carcanet, 2021). His poems have appeared in *The TLS, The White Review* and *Poetry Ireland Review*.

Before We Go Any Further

TRISTRAM FANE SAUNDERS

CARCANET POETRY

First published in Great Britain in 2023 by
Carcanet
Alliance House, 30 Cross Street
Manchester, M2 7AQ
www.carcanet.co.uk

A CIP catalogue record for this book is
available from the British Library.

ISBN 978 1 80017 325 5

Book design by LiteBook Prepress Services
Printed in Great Britain by SRP Ltd, Exeter, Devon

The publisher acknowledges financial
assistance from Arts Council England.

CONTENTS

For Lucia

BEFORE WE GO ANY FURTHER

HOME,

like pigeons do. We follow
the pull of sockets deep
in our thick, wet heads,
our sodden radar: warm,
warmer, colder, warm.
The yearn, that sub- or ultra-
sonic *wumph* from tail
to beak to gut, that hits
whenever we face due you
or you-by-near-enough.
The clunk, that eight- or cue-
ball of yes dropped snug
into the centre pocket
behind the eyes. Half-
recognised, we follow
what recognises us
by the usward trail it lays:
breadcrumb, breadcrumbs, dust.
Guided, or strung along, amazed,
stumbling home. Tug, tug.

I

The glass is falling hour by hour, the glass will fall forever,
But if you break the bloody glass, you won't hold up the weather.

Caligari. Even if
    I'd seen the film
    – no one there had,
except for you, handsome but shy,
  and The Hulk explaining Prynne
in the kitchen doorway to a cornered Harley Quinn –

  your darkened sockets felt-tipped into
      diamond points,
      haunted look
 and turtleneck would always add
 up to nobody's first guess.
Edward Scissorhands without the scissors? Unless

  I'd lied and yelled *Great costume! Yes*
    I'd recognise
    you anywhere
  we never would have met. We slept
  together once, or almost slept.
All night I watched your broken, unplugged TV set

  paint shadows longer than the walls.
    At dawn you cracked
    the blind. Your eyes
  and clanging headache had you running
  straight to the bathroom cabinet.
Charivari comes from *karebaria,*

Greek for migraine, 'heavy head'.
    It's a parade
      of noise and hate,
  rough music, metal banging metal,
   a chorus raised to shame a real
or imaginary figure of disgrace.

  When the angry townsfolk chase
     the dark-eyed man,
      he runs until
  his heart gives out. The final reel
   reveals it's all a dream, the face
belongs to someone else. I still don't know his name.

THE ONEIROSCOPIST
Edith Rimmington, Dulwich Picture Gallery

The diving helmet is a perfect fit.
If anyone could make it work, then it
had to be you, despite the length of this
(tell me the tactful word, Edith – proboscis?)
        this seabird's beak, projecting from the hull
        of your salt-white and pecked-clean seabird skull,
        a plaguemask for the drowning and the dead.
        I dreamt this figurehead became your head.

I like this one, you said. You like the dark,
and birds in galleries, and bones in galleys.
British Surrealism, a Noah's Ark
of you-like animals. I kept a tally.
        Three skeletons on that wall over there
        are you. Six cats. The feathered blue giraffe
        is you. Those crows. The goose with lilac hair.
        I almost said, *I like your soul, your laugh,*

a flood of gush. I would have tried to tell you,
but leaning on this picture frame, we slipped
into its silent world, where words like *soul*
sound too sincere, or else too counterfeit;
        curse words, old oaths to summon up a deluge,
        finding only one of us equipped.
        You're snug and dry inside your soundproof bowl.
        The diving helmet is a perfect fit.

MONKFISH

It'd always be late. High on Red Bull and Blue Planet,
Attenborough levelling her mind, she'd call
me again, still up at four in the morning,
not tearful, just earnest and wired, calling
for no reason, no better reason than to share

her latest newly memorised litany of names.
*Lophius, or monkfish, or fishing frog, or
sea devil.* Revision. Of course she was fine.
She told me, the worst time, that she empathised
with its teeth. *The teeth will become temporarily*

*depressed, so as to offer no impediment
to an object gliding towards the gut.*
God knows why I'd pick up. Pity, or pride
in my own selfless patience? She the seashell
held to my ear, I'd listen then half-listen

like the line I pictured in the air between us;
neutral, intermittent, static. Cagey about being,
but reluctantly talked into it. *The body,
given time and a stable bed, will change
and blend with its surroundings.*

Given time, I thought she'd learn to fit
in, tone down the strangeness,
or even occasionally sleep, to call
someone else, anyone – Samaritans, Nightline,
the talking clock... *standard network rate. Your call*

is a low, keening sound. Your call
is inaudible to divers. Your call
is inaudible to all the undrowned.

SILKWORMS

At 28 I have more pets than friends
and do not give them names. I cut them off,
or try to, when they're too glued to the web
unspooling from whichever of their ends
has means. Their faceless faces look appalled:

a silk pall, peppercorned with tiny leavings,
or starched Elizabethan collar stitched
with fine black pearls, against the velvet blebs
of thick green putty – mulberry chow,
it's all domestic silkworms live on now.

Full of themselves, underground-white and full,
fed up inside their home-spun terminals
at the end of the line, survivors hear a strange,
insistent, tinny voice: *all change, all change.*
(I meant to write to you. I'd like to call.)

As we grow older we forget to talk.
Mermaidlike, the flightless adult moth
to buy its heavy legs has sold its mouth.
Those miracle-white angel wings are props.
They must pick up the beds they are and walk.

HOW THE RAVEN ATE THE MOON

She couldn't tell me past the lump in her throat, but something
was broken, or breaking. It had been four weeks exactly
since she'd stopped taking whatever it was that she'd been taking.

The last white pill was gone and nothing else was working,
so I gave her *How the Raven Ate the Moon*
filled with hot milk, and wrapped her palms around the hollow

eye of it and kept on talking. *In the story,*
Raven has been flying for (I told her) *twenty*
eight long nights and days without a crumb of sleep

or wink of meat. He makes a wager with a sockeye
salmon over which is stronger: human love or...
By the time I'd finished talking, she'd stopped shaking.

Crazed with hairline cracks and chipped, it still holds water
even now. Although it's years since we two split,
I just can't let it go, this tacky mug I bought

in Canada – I've filled it with the sweet and bitter
nettle tea, handpicked, each leaf plucked like a feather
from the black-and-white-and-red unfaded picture

printed across it, of a photo of a painting
by a famous local artist, of a myth
I never learnt. She needed something she could handle,

so I made it up and meant it, every word.
A white lie, like a desperate last-minute gift
picked up before a flight. I brewed it from the floating

scraps that fill my head like weeds, like *lunary
is honesty, unless it's only mugwort*. Like
love, or the other thing. And like a starving bird

she swallowed it. Or made me think she'd swallowed it.

CONTINENTAL DRIFT

On the deep channels late last night, an hour before you left,
I found a documentary called *Continental Drift*.

Abraham Ortelius, in 1596,
saw forms that once belonged, and thought of continental drift.

Theatrum Orbis: a painted world unfurled itself, revealing
heavens of ink and coupled names and continental drift.

Of course, we all know better now. Tectonics with its coloured
arrows pinned to earth the lie of continental drift.

There is no centrifugal pseudo-force, only a slow
subduction. Heat is lost. Plates 'grow' apart, not 'drift'.

As you sealed the final box I failed to meet your eye,
with mine – unmoving, not unmoved – on *Continental Drift*.

FAULT

Some days the salt is closer to the surface.
    It only takes the slightest tilt
for tears to come,
      breaking the meniscus.

        I know how he felt,
      the boy in the story who pressed his thumb
        to the rift in the dam,
      the hairline crack that might become a fault,

while high overhead the ocean or the river,
    cresting the lip of the old defences
unnoticed, had hung there
   a moment, and spilt.

WEATHER ABOUT THE TALKING

Medium-term exposure to the expert's bonhomie
made me want to kill a dachshund. I switched him off

and watched the television's vapours trickle to a halt.
Once the eighteen-hour curfew had been put in place, silence

(though still highly recommended) was no longer compulsory.
So we talked. Filling the time and filling the room.

By early March the vapours took on substance, or colour,
or seemed to. Perhaps our connoisseurship had improved.

Formerly indetectable, we grew to notice
my blue-grey hesitations, the charcoal of your tssks.

Ankle-deep in atmosphere, our cardice lives
were lent, for a while, a certain glam-rock chic.

By June they had repealed the smoking ban.
Trees were invisible at sixty feet.

Things were worse indoors. The basement filled,
the ground floor followed suit. We laughed less. My mist

was complacent and dull, like a brick, or the opposite
of a brick. July, we held a nondenominational burial

for our extractor fan, an honourable defeat.
Your mist had a spine to it, something from the deep.

It was, even with all the windows open,
as reluctant as we were to leave the house.

August and our heads were in the clouds.
We forgot each other's faces, forgot our own.

It wasn't until winter, after months of conversation,
that you tried to look me in the eye again.

Blinded, stumbling in the almost perfect white-out,
we drew breath, and a silence fell like rain.

AGAINST REMINISCENCE

To open memory and find it empty.
    Or open memory and find

nothing worth the finding, or uncover
    something better kept covered, if kept at all,

kept badly, that ought to have been uncovered
    weeks or years ago, now furred

and leaking, shrivelled up,
    unrecognisable. Better to let

the bottle hold its drunken sibyl,
    the sibyl hold her secrets,

secreting what they will,
    disturbing nothing, undisturbed.

HEALTH
Botanic Gardens, Ventnor

What is that? Something honeylike that makes me lean in closer,
a tag in Latin dangling from its neck below the bloom.
Every flower has a stamen – do I mean a stigma? –
at its heart to lure the needle-bearing honeybee
doing its rounds from bed to bed, fretting like a doctor,
looping its indecipherable cursive in the air.

The poster campaign tells us *we must work to fight the stigma*
over mental health but they don't mean that. Health, I mean.
Nobody is angry or ashamed of being healthy.
The rich sea air, my guidebook says, and rising temperatures
mean semi-hardy plants that elsewhere just can't hack the weather
survive the whole year round outside here, kept alive by Ventnor.

All my friends are sick. I love them and I'm scared.
Z is sick. I mean, she's ill. *An ill wind; boding ill.*
The body bodes the way a broken bone can sense the storm,
her every joint an advert for the coming inner weather.
I want to help but all I do is rhyme. Seeking shelter
from the rain that all at once is everywhere and on me,

I turn a corner past the greenhouse, find the blue pagoda.
In it, you are reading this. Hello. Can I sit down?
This is the closest I will ever come to being honest.
Look at the pretty flowers. People died where we are sitting.
Everyone my age is sick. I've never slept beside
someone who didn't need pills to separate the day from night.

Some of them have disappeared. Some wear the stigmata
on the lower inner arm that marks the almost-martyr.
Variegated, reads the metal tag. *Perennial*.
The sky is bleeding white, squeezed dry above the blue pagoda
but the rain keeps coming. That was the other thing. It's why
they made the garden here, after they knocked the old place down.

In a room beside the mushroom house, a TV set repeats
three minutes of a video from 1969:
the BBC had sent a helicopter like a humming
bee to hover near the empty sanatorium,
not yet collapsed. A tracking shot. There's just so much of it,
window after window and an unseen voice explaining

how the lungs would fill with what was held in drops of water.
I'd like to bring them here, my friends, tell them everything
they lie in bed and think of doesn't matter for a while,
that it can wait until they've got their breath back in this shelter
we have made from words. The guidebook mentions that the doctor
who founded Ventnor's institute for sickness of the chest

died here – tuberculosis, yes, despite the warm sea air
and honey in hot water. Is it me or is it getting
darker? Now it's late and I can hardly see the flowers.
Close your eyes and sit with me for just a little longer.
We'll talk about our friends, about the flower and its stigma
till this rain dies down. The guidebook says he tried, the doctor.

The guidebook says it's quiet here, but we can't hear it over
the water falling everywhere and on the blue pagoda.

LULLABY

No one sleeps. Matt living with his parents
again and two days sober, almost. Jackie
taking pictures of the moon
that wakes above the thumbtacked desk
she rests her cheek on when
she inks her picture-books

of pyramids or shapes her careful lines
of coke. It's almost dawn as Zoe starts
another chapter of the niche
erotica she ghosts for seven
cents a word, awake
as us. You look awake.

I look like something you might like to sleep through.
Richard with the man he used to lie
beside, who's on a bed on wheels
and never sleeps or wakes. It's not
what any of us wanted.
Hum it. It will do.

BEFORE WE GO ANY FURTHER

Let's tether our hot, sore hearts
to the post. Tie up our lungs,
leave our breath to catch itself.
Lighter and calmer, we'll walk
up to the crest of this hill
and stop. Place your hands
to my empty chest, knock twice
for luck, for luck, as I raise
mine up under your hair, stroke
the nape of the neck that crooks
to one side as you listen
until we hear nothing beat
slower. Then and only then
will we turn back, hand in hand,
to unhook the soft bronchi
that buck, still hoarse from shouting,
scoop our hearts cool from the trough,
pick up right where we left off.

II

Tis a strange place, this Limbo!—not a Place,
Yet name it so;—

THE SQUAT PEN

rests in the visitor's centre.
Or rather, does not rest
but, surreally, dangles
up in a plastiglass
pillar, moisture-, odour-
and temperature-controlled,
above a digital montage
already showing its age:
green shapes swirl closed, then open.
The poet's squat pen

floats on a nylon string,
hung out to dry, fishing
for nothing, over a C.
G.I. display of Heaney-
inspired video artwork.
At all hours of the clock,
rendered in green, his themes
pulse in uneasy rhythms,
morphing on every off-beat:
a spade becomes a boat,

Busby Berkeley eels
cavort into a cartwheel's
spokes, then blades of grass,
resolutely lifeless.
Drowning in the lime-
light of its perspex column,
it would never write
this lurching squib. Ingrate,
why do I have to sneer?
Why did I even *come* here?

~

To put the truth down simply
we have to let it lie.
Around the corner from
the pen's vivarium
his blotted pages prove it:
an ugly, graceful fight
between the words he wanted
to say and those he said,
writing his 'tongue-tied sorrow'
out of *The Harvest Bow*

to leave a floating silence,
a warm, untroubled space.
Me, I can't stop tugging
at the invisibly thin
line between *true* and *honest*
on which my own words rest,
or hang, in this airless alcove,
trying to tilt toward love
but meeting passing faces
with doubt, a misplaced emphasis.

Between them, muscle mass
and wingspan leave them little room
for tact. Seabirds, blunt
as razors, well used
to the bait-and-snatch.

Bradford Naugler, the Eastern
Seaboard's greatest living sculptor,
has on any given night
no less than twenty wooden gulls
moulting in his shack.

A life's work, to capture
their full bloody-minded range
of unalikeness: hopeful;
cocky; psychopathic; blank.

All beautiful. A reporter
from the Tribune once asked him,
'So, you like seagulls, Bradford?'
Laughter. 'Just a hunch.'

A moment's thought, then: 'No.
No, I guess I love them.
I love these little bastards,
but not much.'

BLANK INSIDE FOR YOUR MESSAGE

Dazzling silver foil
behind a star-shaped hole.

*

The wise men's sandpaper desert
makes your fingers smart.

*

Open: 'Hark! The herald...'
Shepherds sing in the fold.

*

Scratch'n'sniff manger:
blood, musk, myrrh.

*

Numb tongue stuck.
The irresistible lick.

MOST HAUNTED

Which makes me wonder: where's the least?
Would it be ghostless, or,
as I suspect,
a home

to less-than-one? Visits decreased
to once a year, a chore
he might neglect.
Alone

and unobserved, the mortgage leased,
a kind of sinecure,
his circumspect
half-moan

unnoticed by the undeceased.
What's he in mourning for,
his self-respect?
He's shown

no fear of exorcist or priest.
They find him such a bore.
His fledgling spect-
ors flown,

his ghostly family at peace,
and him still here, no longer sure
this shackled act's
his own.

SIX GLIMPSES OF EILEEN AGAR IN A CROWD

Mercury falling in the weatherglass
and rising in the hatter's tinned niçoise.

Commuters part for what they must suppose is,
amid this red-faced sea, a second Moses.

Painted cork and coral, bark and bone.
Uncommon sole's toothed spine: Poseidon's comb.

Your salt-breeze glides above all that's barbaric.
No flies on you, Eileen, you fly agaric.

Dalí doffed his diving helmet; you,
one better, had your hat and ate it, too.

A crest that tips to meet the wave you raise:
Ceremonial Hat for Eating Bouillabaisse.

TUESDAY

The corkboard lake *thtuck-thtuck*s
beneath our golf-shoes. We are now
three days from shore. The sun,
Post-It yellow, is thinly glued
to noon, like the OUT TO LUNCH
on God's glass door. *Thtuck,*
thtuck. We move at a clip, but
some one or thing is gaining.
That wheeled sled a day or half
a day behind us, its trundle
sole subject of our thoughts,
our muffled dreams, soundtrack
to the snatched, unchewable
things we eat on the move.

CURSE

Greg, gently mashing the keys of a Steinway.
Or Greg, brow furrowed, struggling to grasp
a toothbrush, album, cup. Now Greg in bed:
listen for the unconsolable *clop*

that comes each night before his hopeless prayers.
Unhappy Greg, remembering the touch
of things, of people. Of his mother's face.
Has he not suffered? Has he not served his time?

Then we shall help him. Slowly lift your arms
into this poem, into Greg's small room,
into his sleeping body. Take his hooves
and wear them. Look, it's not so bad.

Try to come to terms with them, the hooves.
The uncompromising fact of them,
unfeeling as woodwork. Four uncrackable lumps
of keratin; hard, staccato, blunt.

I wore them for an hour; Greg, for three
whole stanzas. Reader, you will keep them
until the day when, thumbless, you remaster
the knack of how to turn a page.

FIVE SONGS ON A CRUEL INSTRUMENT
translated by AE Pious

Though he published little in his four decades at Y— University, AE Pious inspired generations of students with his passion for the languages and literatures of the British Isles, equally at home with Jèrriais counting-rhymes and Shetlandic folk songs, with Welsh riddles, neo-Latin curses and Cornish shepherds' prayers.

In his lectures, usually given without notes, AEP would sometimes follow a thorny quotation from, say, Old Norse or Scots Gaelic verse with his own off-the-cuff translation, extemporised in fluent rhyming lines – his unforgettable white eyebrows waggling in time with the metre. Sadly, it was only in his final weeks that he began seriously to consider preserving these spirited English versions with a view to publication.

Nevertheless, having resolved to do so, he worked diligently on this project right up until the time of his accident, envisioning a small chapbook of neglected late-medieval texts – many transcribed directly from the manuscripts, to be published in print for the first time – in a facing edition with his lyrical responses. It was to be no mere translation, but a conversation across the centuries with these dead texts, an act of communion, even a rite – as he was overheard to call it – of resurrection. A beautiful idea. One that, on hearing the news, I determined to carry through in his name, as a token, all too late now, of my fondness, and our – I think – unspoken understanding.

It would be regrettable if recent press interest in the nature of AEP's death were to overshadow his life and work. Indeed, I have come to suspect that some of the wilder misreporting is responsible for the abruptness with which every press

I approached rejected his verse – a disappointment, though hardly a surprise, given the controversy-shy timorousness of the current publishing climate. His voice must be *heard*. To ensure it is, I find that I must whisper. I had no choice but covertly to insert these pages – having won the confidence of an insomniac printer who harboured some sympathy for AEP's more esoteric interests – into the manuscripts of nine minor poets published by a Manchester-based press. To those nine who find their books unexpectedly enriched by this small but necessary subterfuge, I offer my sincerest apologies.

I hope that this selection will stand as a tribute to the man I knew, to his meticulous and wide-ranging scholarship, to his talents as a translator and his peculiar but genuine gifts as a lyric poet, long after the headlines have been forgotten. Rather than the facing edition he imagined, here his versions are allowed to stand alone, released from their originals, to sing, as it were, unchained and unchained.

AEP planned for each of his poems to be accompanied by a detailed critical commentary. Though this project was unfortunately still incomplete at the time of the incident, an unfinished note on "Lusus's Hymn" was retrieved unscathed, and is included here as a gesture towards his intended design.
– *Margo Pil, University of Y—, 2023*

THAT DARK HARP
Angl. Sax. Ballad, Cantab MS A XV

'As a crab has a claw,
    As a hawk has a craw,
And an asp's sharp jaw
      Has a fang,

As a plan has a flaw,
    As a plank had a saw,
And a bad man, by law,
      Always hangs,

As a path has a track,
    Atlas has a bad back,
And a blank has a lack,
      Alarms rang

At my fall, my fall...
    My chasm's black walls
Shrank — away crawl
      My gang.

As a wasp always swarms,
    And man's wrath always harms,
My harp's always warm,'
      Satan sang.

LLEWELLYN

Welsh elegy, selected verses

When Llewellyn bled, the cherry grew red,
the elder-tree berry grew sweet.

When he slept, the velvet leveret
nestled by Llewellyn's feet.

When Llewellyn wept, tempests swept
the welded, eel-grey sky.

The slyest elves resembled themselves
when held by Llewellyn's eye.

Llewellyn's green cheeks swelled the dry leeks
when he fell, feebly fevered.

When Llewellyn fell, the steeple bells
were empty. Hell cheered.

FINDING KILNICKY
Irish drinking jig

If living is dying,
If singing is sighing,
If kicking pricks is tricky,
  Try living in Kilnicky!
  Why, try living in Kilnicky!

If thick is thin,
If kissing is sin,
If this stick insists it's sticky,
  Try living in Kilnicky!
  Tris, try living in Kilnicky!

If thinking is tiring,
By 'Nicky's inspiring
Skinny limbs jig hicky-dicky,
  Try living in Kilnicky,
  Kids, try living in Kilnicky!

Dry lips will drink,
Blind lids will blink
In its light – this bright sky-city!
  Living in Kilnicky, Christ
  Is living in Kilnicky.

Its chill wind winds
In childish minds,
Twisting ill wits sickly:
  Sip this gin, Jim, slip right in.
  Kilnicky, Kilnicky, Kilnicky

WYCH BROOK
Old Scots, from 'Lost Folk Songs of Troon, Vol. O'

My smooth brook knows
No storm-blown sky,
No flood to drown,
Nor drooth to dry,

No owl to hoot,
Nor flock to throng.
On old Wych Brook
Look not too long.

No goby swoops,
Try not thy hook;
Worms only rot
On old Wych Brook.

From Wych Brook's slop
Grow rocks of gold.
My worldly goods,
Soon got, soon sold.

Row north, my son,
By soft moonglow,
To cold Wych Brook,
By frost, by snow.

Go soon, my son,
By strong wood prow.
Don't stop, nor stoop
To mop my brow.

To go's to know
Wych Brook's own cost:
Blood, my son,
My fool, my loss.

LUSUS'S HYMN
UK, unsung

'Thy usury…' Just church's humdrum murmur.
Just stuffy hymns, hum-sung by ugly husks.
Just myth wrung dry. Just stuff: pyx, crypt, urn, myrrh.
Rust-junk. Spurn churchful *mustn't*'s musty musk.
Fuck dull, try cult. Try *subkultur*. Burn sulphur.
Shun sun – try sulky, susurrusful dusk.
Try drunk, unruly, druggy, lustful Lusus.
Trust us, just us. Cry Lusus! Lusus! Lusus!

Lusus's unjustly dusty truths,
Dug up by us, usurp dry church's rhythms.
Unbury fun! Thump guru-drums, strum crwths
Subtly strung by sunburnt nymphs. Myth hums.
Succubus trysts! Such sylphs! Such sky-flung Crus!
Sup cupfuls, jugfuls – Lusus's ur-zythums!
Thrust up full lungs, cry Lusus! Lusus! Lusus!
Lusus!
        Lusus!
                Lusus!
   Lusus!
                      Lusus! [1]

---

[1] AEP: While the first four of these *Five Songs* are, of course, variants of familiar folk tunes (see appendix), *Lusus's Hymn* is something different: as far as I have been able to ascertain, this is the first time it has been rendered into modern English. This is perhaps surprising, as though the Bodleian MS is faded and, in places, charred, the text is perfectly legible – as is the curious injunction, added by a later hand, that it should remain 'unsung'. The ottava rima of this version is intended as an homage to Luís de Camões's *Lusiads*. Though the influence of Celtic religions from Britain on

the Iberian peninsula – and vice versa – is well documented
(cf. Pious, " 'Unshriven, In Their Footsteps Follow I': Gael-Force
Winds in Andorra", *Journal of Classical and Sacred Philology*, 1983),
Lusus's Hymn may be the only extant evidence of a cult in Sub-
Roman Britain dedicated to Lusus, a malign and anarchic minor
god of temptation and debauchery – a 'friend of savage man'
(cf. Camões), son of Bacchus and provincial deity of Lusitania,
or modern-day Portugal – a cult which appears to have vanished
without a

My fan is utterly devoted and the only one I have, though whether this is proof of my success or failure is a point on which we disagree. My fan gives me a lavish gift each time we meet, or did, at least, the only time we met,

under a railway arch in South-East London, where they handed me a scarf of such untarnishable beauty that I knew I'd never take it off, so I have never tried it on. My fan curates (or 'edits') a small magazine – I don't recall

the name – which published my translations of my subtle early poems into the style of my more plangent and meticulously detailed later poems, in its first and as yet only issue, underneath a sonnet by a soap actor from Wales.

My fan is disapproved of by my current lover, who distrusts all fans in general, understandably, given their years of working as a junior literary agent opening parcels sent by fans of X, such as the six-by-eight-foot black and white painting of Letchworth as seen from the sky which came for X while they were living in a ten-by-twelve-foot caravan and now is hanging on our bedroom wall. My fan writes little poems of their own. They're just the kind of poems they *would* write, or so

I gather, never having read them. If my fan should read this poem, and they will, they will around this line begin to feel an itch of disappointment, and a faint suspicion that this poem's 'flaws' are all, in fact, *devices* calibrated to

provoke that feeling in them, and in them alone, a kind of metrical deterrent, not unlike the shrill, inaudible alarm that wards off dogs and adolescents, a faint suspicion which will drag its heels towards a dim awareness that, despite

its tenderness and charm, this *is* an act of violence – and will love it all the same.

THE MEDIUM

*Cinema was embraced as a medium that produced ghostlike
moving images; it was, accordingly, enlisted in psychic research.*

– John Potts, 'Ghost-Hunting in the 21ˢᵗ Century'

That Bogart scene. He's in the rain, of course,
locked out and pushing every goddamn button.
The intercom is silent. Nothing gives,
till all at once these overlapping voices

crackle through the night, the single speaker.
is that is who are you who's with you come
They hear each other, fooled. The door clicks open.
And in this way we misdirect the dead.

Cigarette burns, hair in the gate, that coarse
hiss? Listen. To stitch a missing button,
it helps to lose your thread. Like *this*. It gives
a certain verisimilitude to voices

live or pre-recorded if the speaker
is level with the heart. And if you come
to interrupt the dead, if you would open
their bricked-up hearts, then imitate *their* dead:

become the voice of their own long-lost cause,
their mute regrets and longings. Find the button
to push, and push it. The recent late don't give
a damn for you, your questions. The only voices

they want to hear are their own absent speakers
a generation further off, and they have come
to wait for their forgiveness, in the open
space behind the screen. Unspeakable, unsaid.

BARABAJAGAL

The hurdy-gurdy man came by last week.
He looked more tired than usual.
There was dust on his jeans, and what may have been
chicken's blood. Just a guess.

i'm depressed, he began, as always.
I offered him a biscuit.
i feel like there are no chances any more
he said, dunking the biscuit.

like even the revolving doors are locked
like i fell asleep in a matinee
and woke up three murders and two marriages later
and all the actors' faces are too close

i feel (he paused to sip) *like a ghost*
I began to explain that it had been
a busy morning and that Sophie
would be back soon from the shops

and could he possibly–? His eye met mine. I stopped.
His dufflecoat shuffled like corn husks
as he stood to put it on, shoulders hunched,
a lizard climbing into last year's skin,

beautiful and old and hardened and diminished.
With one foot through the doorway, he looked back:
you were the last. He left his drink unfinished.
He has not returned.

ALIEN VS JAWS

The next shot is a nod to *Predator*,
as Michael Caine's besnorkled diving mask
investigates a row of – are they eggs?
Under the bladderwrack, cucumberlike,
alive. Cue music. Mask, pod, mask, pod, mask.
You know the rest. His bubbles make no sound.
It's hours before they even break the surface.

Now crossfade slowly to *ext: elsewhere* – where
scriptdoctor Kay sits ashenfaced behind
a softly singing Remington Remette.
Screws loose, it chimes each time she strikes the keys,
humming her name in its one cold clear note,
as clear and cold as what's now left of Michael,
his guts and innards – all but the heart – translucent,

more jellyfish than man, the bones licked clean,
it seems, from *inside* their glassy, skin-thin sacklet.
Only the deep-red heart (too deep) still moves
and moves more quickly than expected. Lithe,
swift and unmoored, it tours his limbs' canals,
looking for all the world like Kay's first goldfish
the day her mother won it from the fair,

trussed in its plastic bag, all waterbound
and waterfilled and clear and waterweight.
Kay types the words *we wait*. So wait. The heart
floats up for seven timelapsed days, shucked skin
forgotten far below. This blown rose bleeds
to white in the air, a dried-up ball of paper

tossed from Kay's fingers as they turn to feathers.

III

I do not find all this absurdity people talk about.
Perhaps a paradise, a serious paradise where lovers hold hands
and everything works.
I am not sentimental.

THE SPHINX
Crystal Palace Park

It's lunch, and I've one leg on either side
of the brick-red haunch. Astraddle, or astride.
A flask on his flank, a sandwich where the spine
would lie, if either of us liars had one,

hindlegs before me and the fore behind.
Although it's true we don't see eye-to-eye
(uneager for the future, I'll keep mine
fixed on what for him's already gone)

we've this in common: neither will admit
we're going nowhere. Someone taught him 'sit'
in 1854. He mastered it.
The hand that framed this fearful symmetry

made something less the bane of Thebes than kith
to Clifford, Big Red Dog. The hieroglyphs
say nothing: LOREM IPSUM DOLOR SIT
in Middle Kingdom script. The riddle's why

the hell we're here, red-faced. Him? Blame the eye
of Mr Jones, first pharaoh of primary
colours when London's walls and tastes and skies
were grey. Me? I've been struggling to cope.

The thermos spirals open with a sigh.
Pandora's dog-red lunchbox will be empty,
the lone and level sandwich gone. Still, why
not give the box a shake. It sounds like hope.

THE HEAD
Crystal Palace Park

In the middle of a lockdown, I am lost
in the living maze. The hornbeam hedge, unminded
now for months, remembering its lopped

limbs, grew headstrong. Wildering, it blinded
its own eye, sewed shut the famous rings,
turning against the maker that designed it.

Turning again, each path re-roots to bring
me, though I hardly mind, to the same dead
end. I have forgotten everything

but these three things: the root of *Penge*, the head
-less sculpture loitering outside the maze,
and one more piece of what I'd always said

was useless trivia, which means three ways,
a forking road, the point where lost begins.
Lost in the mid-Eighties, it was Dante's,

the head. I'd like to think it wore a grin.
Penceat: from the Welsh for 'head' and 'wood'.
Whichever way I turn leads further in.

The statue's standing where Penge Place once stood,
demolished for that looking-glass, the Palace,
whose weightless walls shine like they never could

when it existed. Living backwards, Alice,
has one advantage in it, said the Queen.
I don't remember it. Pre-emptive malice?

Or knowing that we're where we've always been,
that turning back does not mean losing ground?
I like it here. I'm lost but hell it's green.

Green as a thought, and no-one else around,
which re-minds me. Trivia can mean
common place; something easily found.

THE BOWL
Crystal Palace Park

The pond beside the Bowl we call the 'rusty laptop'
has grown to be less pool than baize pool-table top.

A moorhen foots it, Christlike, but for the red dot
that's more a mark of Cain. A football floats to a stop.

It's reached the stage now where to reach the stage is a hop
from the always greener side where grass is smoked and cropped

to plant both feet on concrete, almost falling in
love with what was. What is a shelter from the wind,

for watching birds – a hawk, a stonechat, crows, the thin
strut of a heron – watching out for needles and tins,

once hosted Gil Scott-Heron, Stone the Crows, and Hawkwind
opening (I swear to God) for Vera Lynn

at a gala fundraiser for – I mean, against – heroin
where the band were reunited with their top

-less Irish go-go dancer, Stacia. These days, Stacia
– an artist, trained in '89 at Hamburg Frei Kunstschule –

makes sense of life by mingling *inner landscapes* and nature.
She grinds up *people, movement, animals* etc.,

into the mix. My laptop's on her Wikipedia.
Like bowerbirds, we gather things that mean together.

Some things go on. The moorhen is a thing that goes
on, not in. Some things just pose and juxtapose

and never break the surface. Some things seem to choose
inertia, having flown, not fallen, out of use.

The Bowl is empty and the Bowl is full. Suppose
I put you in this scene? Suppose that you refuse?

I'd like to think there's time for unbilled cameos,
late entrances, green shoots against rust-red, a future

arrives – as parakeets – to say the stage is yours,
Lucia. Green feathers burst into applause.

THE DINOSAUR
Crystal Palace Park

The iguanodon,
       like everyone,
            is guesswork.

Apologetic plaques
       correct the too-
            long necks,

imagined horns, and all-
       round lack of feathers.
            Whatever,

we like them wrong. Henry,
       these were made
            for you

to hide from. *We must walk,*
       you tell me, *very*
            quietly.

We are protected by
       a moat, and a fence
            waist-high

to me, head-high to you,
       and ankle-high
            to them.

Across the water, *he*
       is hiding too.
            Bashful,

tail toward us, snout
        nuzzling the ground
                for bones.

The time-pressed sculptor, knowing
        how little was known –
                they'd what,

a kneecap, teeth, one shin
        to go on? – sighed
                and turned

the doubtful face from view,
        a little abstract
                in the concrete.

Dickens stood here, saw
        the megalosaur,
                went home

and wrote *Bleak House*. You draw
        a book for me:
                T-Rex,

in his blue cape, breathes fire.
        Dicynodon
                looks on.

I know that I should draw
        a lesson here,
                something

about their need to cobble what they could into a whole,
brushing away the dust and counting feet. Tapping, tapping.
Our common work of making something old from something new.

I'd draw a lesson here,
        but it's summer.
                Lessons

are centuries away.
        Look over there,
                no, higher,

where the giant sloth
        (my favourite)
                is hunting

imagined concrete ants
        inside a concrete
                tree.

When you're old enough
        to read these words,
                you won't.

Explorer, you will find
        better things
                to dig through.

TREBLE AND CLEF

Your two white rats. The cage arrived before them,
inch for inch a palace. Four storeys of amusements:
ladders, boltholes, ice-cube trays for feed and fruit.
Clef I liked best. Her parrot act, clinging

to my shoulder as I padded round the flat.
She'd sit and stare at nothing, squeaking like the toys
she wouldn't touch. While you were gone she gave up breathing,
spent six months in the bottom of the freezer

till your return. In spring we buried her,
shoveling with a spoon in Crystal Palace Park,
taking turns to keep a lookout for the keeper,
working in shifts, watching each other's back.

THIS FLY IN MY EAR

My one good lug against the coffee-table,
my father's muttered comfort burbles
thickly through the vegetable oil:
We'll drown the bugger, float him out. Hold still.

It had slipped the nets, the zap-o-mats, the spiders,
to dance this brittle little tarantella
on my bones; my ear its *bodhrán,* tripping
the dark, fantastically unconcerned.

At the table, I am patient, weighing
each viscous thought with care, calm
as a Volvo at a filling-station, until
something unexpected bubbles up:

what if all this was planned? Perhaps it knew
the ins and outs – perhaps it swotted, gleaned
a thing or two about the cochlea,
the ossicles and incus, found the oval window

ajar, and burrowed in. Perhaps.
Later, in the shower, I never saw
a body circling the plughole, never
felt for certain something giving way.

SUNCREAM

This unique dual-ribbon formula
binds us to one another. It *combines*
strong protection with luxurious

hydrating silk that falters from your shoulders.
In the late sun, hung from seabreeze, your delicious
sweat—*octocrylene, alcohol, aqua,*

glycerine—causes something to ignite
around my helpless fingertips—*parfum.*
All these months on, *phenoxyethanol*

still rising from the blistered ashes,
our cornucopia of *passiflora*
incarnata extract finds its tongue

in gestures, silent jargon. Next to you
those few words I knew lost all their meaning.
Linalool, beloved, *linalool.*

CLUE

Peccable timing had me caught red-handed.
You gasped and shuddered, reached for the lead piping,
the candlestick, the rope, whatever came

to hand. When it was done, this perfect game,
we found ourselves fastidiously wiping
away the fingerprints we'd somehow branded

painlessly across our backs in blood.
Your blood, Miss Scarlet. Ask Professor Plum
(making reference to the periodic)

how something elemental as this trick
of moonlight, nature's rulebook, could become
taboo, or seen as anything but good.

CLUB ANTICHRIST

Polite and studded, fearsomely polite, the misfits fit
into each other like ballgag in mouth, or unkind words
in other mouths elsewhere than here. For here we find The Cure,
Sisters of Mercy in the next room on, and in the next
a man roped into acting out the stripped-back semaphore
for 'I'm St Andrew and these Achaeans have taken against me.'

With every lick of her bullwhip's tip to the blushing meat
of Andrew's thigh, her glasses mist a little more. Sex
is a word; shame, a label; Antichrist, a word on labels
on hangers in the vinyl cloakroom. In the final vision
of Daniel, He might be 'a little horn'. For lovers whose x
sports the mark of something hard to beat, 'a little horny'

sits uncomfortably. Here is something pure. The shy urge,
centred. The meek will, inherent. Kingdom come, secure.

BONFIRE

Battersea Park

A befuddled, absent mayor takes the credit
for the blaze that upstages each year's fireworks.
For the scorched grass, the inarticulate woodsmoke
that both damps and dries the tearful, toasted
faces of the cold-toed huddle in their hats.
Bonfire, *bon chance, bon nuit*. My hands
in your pockets, your hair in my face.
Like a beating toffee apple, my heart in your mouth.

UNDER
after Jonas Hanway

My love, come on in out of the outdoors
into a room whose walls are beaded curtains,
whose roof relies on one supporting beam,
whose swift collapse is all but guaranteed.

We'll let whoever's taller take in hand
the rain-black, wordless question of its curved
cedilla handle. Listen to its Morse;

O kettledrum for drunk percussionists!
O wandering gazebo, wayward tent!

Look up, my love. We'll scry its nylon starmap –
the constellations Spoke and Spoke and Spoke
bespeak a world of worse alternatives.

Yonder – the walking damp, and those who turn
to unarticulated surrogates,
unfashionable hats, etc.

Behold the phantom of a headless man,
his collar yanked up over his wet hair,
sleeves flapping like an unloved spaniel's ears…

But pity more the wretched few caught short
with only, say, a newspaper for shelter,
or, worst of all, a single sheet of paper –

what good's a page against the whole damn world?

But if you're ever under, *really* under,
nothing between you and the falling sky,
beloved, take this poem. Hold it up
like you hold me, that it may lead you,
        however far it's able,
                homeward, dry.

THE KEY

A glass harmonica is not a harmonica
    and only half glass, full
of nothing
    to the wetted brim,
each chime
    the gift

of half a drop of water which, in this weird aria,
    is for a moment thicker
than blood.
    Lammermoor,
this stammered
    l'amour

is not the melody I used to sing.
    Lucia,
for years I was running
    the taps till everything ran clear and cold,
running a finger round the rim
    of every line, listening

for the right ring.
    The tune I played was crystalline, controlled.
It was a lifeless thing.
    The living key
is the one you sing,
    the note that's true.

Benjamin Franklin,
    nine years before inventing
the glass harmonica,
    unearthed it too.
It calls for risk, a little luck,
    a blinding light. It is

the iron and the tether
    and the thing in flight above.
The right key, reader, is
    that word you're thinking of,
and it will let you play
    with lightning.

A week before my twenty-first,
it arrived. Your gift for every occasion:

The Oxford Book of English Verse
Sir Arthur Quiller-Couch Edition

Wide for First Class, its green weight forced
through the letterbox tore the wrapping open.

I'd half expected it. Of course
the same book. The same dedication.

You gave it to my mother first,
for some anniversary, now forgotten.

I found it after the divorce,
and would read it often,

skipping the first page every time.
with love, from me to you

in your thin scrawl, a snagged line
of her favourite Beatles tune,

your first dance, above a rhyme
for an eight-centuries-dead cuckoo.

Early bird and earworm tied
like a joke, or something true.

Foolish, inseparable. Why
not, for a gift, forgive you?

It's April 1st. I crack the spine
and watch the words spring new:

Sumer is icumen in
lhude sing cuccu

ACKNOWLEDGEMENTS

Versions of these poems previously appeared in *Poetry London*, *Oxford Poetry*, *Agenda*, *The Luxembourg Review*, *New Poetries VIII* (Carcanet), *Five Songs on a Cruel Instrument* (Broken Sleep / Legitimate Snack), *The Interpreter's House*, *And Other Poems*, *bath magg*, *The Fortnightly Review*, *PN Review* and *The Moth*. Thanks are due to their editors.

Further thanks to: Astrid, Katy, Sasha and everyone in their workshops, where several of these poems were written; the keen-eyed early readers I've inflicted poems upon, including Ali, Abi, Camille, Don, Luke and Nell; my mother, my father and my sister.

I'm grateful to everyone at Carcanet, particularly the indefatigable Michael Schmidt for two years of politely asking me if I had a book yet, and to my editor John McAuliffe (*miglior fabbro*, fabulous mingler) for forcing me to stop taking things out, then encouraging me to sit down and write some poems. You provide the forecast, John, and I'll make up the weather.

This book, like its author, is for Lucia Morello.